Now You're COOKING
HEALTHY RECIPES FROM LATIN AMERICA

CUBA

Kayleen Reusser

PURPLE TOAD
PUBLISHING

P.O. Box 631
Kennett Square, Pennsylvania 19348
www.purpletoadpublishing.com

Now You're COOKING

HEALTHY RECIPES FROM LATIN AMERICA

Brazil

Cuba

Guatemala

Mexico

Puerto Rico

Printing   1   2   3   4   5   6   7   8   9

Publisher's Cataloging-in-Publication Data
Reusser, Kayleen
   Now You Are Cooking: Cuba / Kayleen
Reusser
      p. cm.—(Now you're cooking. Healthy
recipes from Latin America)
Includes bibliographic references and index.
ISBN: 978-1-62469-040-2 (library bound)
1. Cooking, Cuban. 2. Cooking—Juvenile
literature. 3. Recipes for health.   I. Title.
 TX716.C8 2013
  641.597291—dc23
                                        20139306074

eBook ISBN: 9781624690419

Printed by Lake Book Manufacturing, Chicago, IL

CONTENTS

Introduction
Hay Que Inventar ("You Have to Be Creative")

Since 1492 when Christopher Columbus discovered the Caribbean island of Cuba, the people of Cuba have lived by the saying, "Hay que inventar," or "You have to be creative." Many times they have done so in order to survive.

Columbus claimed Cuba in honor of Spain. The Spanish people assumed ownership of the island located almost 100 miles south of Florida and slightly smaller than the state of Pennsylvania. During Spain's rule, black slaves were brought from Africa to work in mines and on plantations. This mingling resulted in a Spanish and African influence on Cuban culture.

As Spanish settlers arrived in Cuba, they brought with them oranges, lemons, rice, and vegetables. They grew sugar cane, which became a major Cuban crop. African slaves, though unable to bring items with them to Cuba, developed a taste for fruits and vegetables like maize (corn), okra, and yuca (cassava) and developed their own recipes. Eventually the Spanish and African cultures joined to create popular Cuban dishes like *Moros y Cristianos* (rice and beans), *arroz con pollo* (chicken with rice), and flan.

Other visitors in the late 1800s and early 1900s came from England, Portugal, and North America. This constant movement of people, culture, and ideas created a blend of culture and recipes that is distinctly

Gulf of
Mexico

Florida
(U.S.)   Miami

Key
West   Straits Of
            Florida

Nassau

**Sierra de Los
Organos**   **Havana**   **Bahamas**

            Matanzas   Santa   Arch. de
            Colon Clara   Sabana

Pinar   Gulfo de
del Río   Batabano

            Cienfuegos   Arch. de
Isla de la   Ciego   Camaguey
Juventud   Trinidad   de Avila

Cuba   Camaguey

125 mi   Holguin
                        Las Tunas
125 km   Arch. de le
            Reina   Manzanillo   Cauto R.

Georgetown **Cayman   **Sierra Maestra**   Baracoa
            Islands
            (UK)**   **Pico
                     Turquino**   Santiago   Guantanamo
                                  de Cuba   Bay

Caribbean
Sea   **Jamaica**

            Kingston

Atlantic
Ocean

**Turks &
Caicos
(UK)**

Cayman Trench

Hai

Port-au-Princ

The food of Cuba is a
combination of tastes
from many continents.

Cuban—spicy and full of life. Over the years it has become impossible to say exactly when or where many Cuban dishes originated. It doesn't matter. Each Cuban cook's desire to add a special touch to traditional recipes has added a new creative dimension.

This freedom of expression changed in 1959 when Fidel Castro took over leadership of Cuba. He established a form of government called Communism. For decades the people of Cuba lived with rations of food, fuel, and other items under Communist rule. To make up for the food shortage many Cubans created gardens around their homes. Some people farmed on government-issued land. Unfortunately, the money farmers earned by selling crops was less than what was needed for the tools and labor needed to start farms.

Fearing Castro's restrictions, thousands of Cubans fled Cuba for the United States and other places where people could live as they wished.

In 2008, Castro resigned his position and his younger brother, Raul Castro, assumed leadership of the country. Thankfully, living conditions in Cuba improved somewhat. Cubans opened restaurants and snack bars and visitors to the island brought food and other goods. Fishing, sugar and coffee growing, and cattle raising are the main food industries of Cuba. Potatoes and rice are grown as well as vegetables and fruits. Still, Cuban people must import many of the items they consume.

Through all of the centuries of hardship, Cubans have learned to be resourceful. 'Hay que inventar' applies to every facet of their lives, including the invention of new Cuban dishes. As you will see, the results are wonderful!

The beauty of a farm in Cuba, where milk cows walk along a dirt road.

Soups and Side Dishes

Moros y Cristianos

Black beans and rice is the most popular food dish in Cuba. Many Cuban cooks would not consider a meal complete without it on the table. In almost every Cuban household a pot of black beans is simmering on the stove, either soupy or thick, ready to feed a hungry family.

The translation of Moros y Cristianos is 'Moors and Christians.' The dish got its name from a time in Spain hundreds of years ago when the Moors (Muslims) and Christians lived as neighbors before the Spanish Inquisition. Black beans are native to Central and South America and rice was introduced to Cuba by the Spanish.

When choosing whether to use dried or canned beans, keep in mind that dried beans expand to double their original size when soaked.

Ingredients

1   small onion, peeled and diced
2   cups long grain rice, cooked
1   15-oz can black beans, drained and rinsed
    olive oil to drizzle

Directions

1. Have **an adult** heat onion in sauce pan over low heat. Add black beans.
2. Cook for five minutes until heated. Stir in rice and cook a few more minutes until heated through. Serve in bowl drizzled with olive oil.

Gazpacho
with Salsa and Croutons

Gazpacho is a chilled soup thought to have roots in Spain, particularly in the cities of Cordoba and Seville. It is traditionally made of bread, olive oil, vinegar, and garlic. As is true with most Cuban recipes, gazpacho can be made with different ingredients including avocados, cucumbers, parsley, watermelon, grapes, meat stock, seafood, and other ingredients. Gazpacho is especially popular in Caribbean countries because it is served cold. On days when temperatures soar a refreshing serving of Gazpacho can be tasty!

Ingredients for Soup

1   12-oz can diced tomatoes or 2 small fresh tomatoes, finely chopped
1   green pepper, deseeded and chopped
1   cucumber, peeled and chopped
1   hardboiled egg, shelled and sliced
12 slices white bread, crusts removed and soaked for 10 minutes in tomato juice
1   chopped onion
1   tablespoon minced garlic
⅓   cup tomato ketchup
1   teaspoon sugar substitute
1   tablespoon paprika
½   cup olive oil
4   tablespoons red wine vinegar

Ingredients for Salsa

2   tomatoes, peeled and diced
½   green pepper, diced
¼   cucumber, peeled, deseeded, diced
½   red onion, diced

Ingredients for Crouton Garnish

6 tablespoons croutons
2 tablespoons toasted almonds
   olive oil

Directions

1. Have **an adult** blend soup ingredients in food processor or blender until smooth. Pour into a large bowl and chill in refrigerator for 30 minutes.
2. Mix ingredients for salsa in a small bowl.
3. Pour gazpacho in individual bowls. Arrange salsa on top. Add croutons and toasted almonds. Drizzle with olive oil.

Cooked Rice

Rice is one of the mainstays in the Cuban diet, and the country has become the biggest consumer of rice in the Caribbean. Many rice dishes include sofrito, a slow-cooked sauce of olive oil, tomatoes, bell peppers, onions, ham, and garlic. It can vary from mild to somewhat spicy. Brown rice contains more nutrients than white rice; when using it, double the cooking time.

Ingredients

7   cups chicken broth (fat-free canned varieties can be used)
4   cups uncooked rice

Directions

1. Mix rice with chicken broth in covered 3-quart saucepan.
2. Bring to boil, then quickly reduce heat to low, cover, and cook until rice is thoroughly cooked and most broth has been absorbed (about 20 minutes). Spoon into serving bowls.

Sofrito is a slow-cooked sauce of olive oil, tomatoes, bell peppers, onions, ham, and garlic that often accompanies rice.

Cuban Salad

Many Cubans grow gardens; therefore, much of their dining consists of fresh fruits and vegetables. This salad is popular at parties because the ingredients can be plucked from the vine right before eating. Use this recipe for a base, then add other ingredients to create your own dish. Remember to record the recipe.

Ingredients

2   ripe red tomatoes, cut into wedges
1   white onion, sliced thin
1   head lettuce, torn in pieces
6   radishes, sliced thin
1   tablespoon minced garlic
¼   teaspoon pepper
½   cup olive oil
¼   cup white vinegar
¼   cup fresh lime juice

Cubans even add avocado

Directions

1. Toss together tomatoes, onion, lettuce, and radishes. Place in refrigerator to chill.
2. Mix garlic with pepper.
3. Pour olive oil, vinegar, and lime juice into a small bowl. Add garlic mixture and stir thoroughly with a spoon or have an adult use a blender.
4. Just before serving toss salad with a large fork and drizzle with dressing.

Cucumbers, oranges, and
peppers grown in gardens offer
Cuban people healthy, low-cost
ingredients for recipes.

Tomato Salad

In Cuba many residents who live in cities have gardens. An urban garden, *organopónicos,* means the food is eaten where it is grown—inside cities. This type of agriculture developed as an essential way of finding food during the 1950s when there was no gas to transport food.

Today, urban gardens are role models for the world. This salad is a standard in many Cuban homes as it is easy to prepare, economical, and delicious.

Ingredients

½ cup olive oil
1   cup diced red onion
1   tablespoon minced garlic
⅓ cup lemon juice
1   green pepper, seeds removed and cut into wedges
4   large red tomatoes, sliced thin

Directions

1. Have **an adult** heat olive oil in 2-quart saucepan until moderately hot, about 300°F.
2. Toss in onion, garlic, and lemon juice. Immediately remove pan from heat and stir constantly for 2 minutes.
3. Cool, then chill in refrigerator.
4. Blanch green pepper by putting it into glass bowl, cover, and microwave on high for 45 seconds.
5. Arrange tomatoes and green pepper on salad plate.
6. Just before serving, stir dressing to blend oil and lemon juice. Lightly drizzle tomatoes and pepper with dressing.

Yuca
with Grapefruit
and Orange Sauce

Yuca is a root vegetable commonly used in Cuban kitchens as potatoes are in American kitchens. Most Americans have eaten yuca without knowing it. Have you eaten tapioca? All tapioca products come from yuca. Another name for yuca is cassava. Yuca (or cassava) flour is used in cooking as a thickening agent. The combined taste of oranges, lime, and grapefruit gives yuca a light, sunny taste.

Ingredients

2   pounds yuca, peeled, quartered, cut into 2-inch chunks
1   tablespoon minced garlic
    juice of 1 lime
¼   cup finely chopped cilantro
½   cup olive oil
2   oranges, peeled and diced
1   grapefruit, peeled and diced
1   large sweet yellow onion, sliced thin

Directions

1. Have an adult boil 6 quarts of water in large pot. Add yuca, bring back to boil.
2. Reduce heat to low and simmer uncovered for 50 minutes or until yuca is tender. Set yuca aside to cool, but don't drain.
3. Mix garlic, lime juice, and cilantro.
4. Have **an adult** heat olive oil in small saucepan until hot, but not smoking (about 300°F). Remove pan from heat.
5. Pour lime juice/garlic/cilantro mixture into hot oil, whisking constantly for 2 minutes.
6. Add oranges, grapefruit, and onion to saucepan and simmer over medium heat, stirring constantly, until onion has lost crispness (about 10 minutes).
7. Drain yuca. Gently toss yuca with fruit salsa and serve.

Yuca is a popular starchy
vegetable grown in Cuba
and used in many fruit
dishes.

Main Dishes
Arroz con Pollo

Arroz con pollo (chicken with rice) is a classic dish served in Cuba, but other Caribbean countries love the combination of flavors as well. You should feel like a true Cuban after preparing this recipe!

Ingredients

1   3-pound chicken, cut in serving-size pieces
½   cup lime juice
1   teaspoon minced garlic
6   tablespoons vegetable oil
1   green pepper, deseeded, chopped
1   white onion, chopped
½   cup raisins
2   bay leaves
1   cup tomato sauce, canned
4   cups chicken broth
2   cups rice
2   cups frozen green peas, cooked

Directions

1. Place chicken in shallow bowl. Using pastry brush cover chicken with lime juice and garlic. Cover and refrigerate 30 minutes.
2. Have an adult heat two tablespoons of oil in skillet or Dutch oven over medium-high heat. Add chicken and brown on both sides, 8 minutes per side. Add more oil as needed. Remove browned chicken and drain on paper towels.
3. Add green pepper, onion, raisins, bay leaves, tomato sauce, broth, and rice to skillet. Mix well and bring to boil over high heat. Reduce heat to simmer, return chicken pieces to mixture, cover, and cook for 25 minutes until chicken and rice are done. Remove from heat and discard bay leaves. Sprinkle with peas and serve from skillet.

Arroz con Pollo is fast and easy to cook, making it a popular dish in Cuba.

Cuban Sandwich

No one is certain where and when the Cuban sandwich was invented. Some people believe it was created in the 1880s by Cuban factory workers who wanted a quick, tasty meal. During the next several decades this delicious recipe made its way to Miami and farther north to New York, New Jersey, and Chicago. The Cuban sandwich is famous for its unique ingredients and preparation. It is usually made with ham, Swiss cheese, pickles, mustard, and Cuban bread. Chicken can be used for a healthier version than the original's ham. The bread can be lightly buttered or brushed with olive oil. The sandwich is pressed flat to melt the cheese and cut into diagonal halves before serving.

A similar sandwich is the medianoche or "midnight" sandwich. It earned its name because people who had spent an evening at the movies would order it in restaurants afterward. It contains the same ingredients as a Cuban sandwich but is made on a sweeter bread called challah.

Ingredients

2   pounds roasted chicken, sliced
½   pound Swiss cheese, sliced
     French bread
     dill pickles, sliced
     yellow mustard (optional)
     mayonnaise (optional)

Note: Allow your chicken and cheese to come to room temperature for 30 minutes before preparing this dish. This will help the cheese melt and prevent the bread from burning.

Directions

1. Have **an adult** preheat griddle or large frying pan to low heat. Lightly grease griddle.
2. Cut bread into sections about 8-inches long. Cut these in half and spread butter on both halves.
3. Layer ingredients on half of the bread slices (butter sides out) in this order: pickles, chicken, and cheese.

The Cuban sandwich gained fame in the United States as a quick, tasty meal.

4. Place slices with chicken on griddle, butter side down. Cover with remaining slices, butter side out. Flatten tops of each sandwich with a large, flat heavy item, such as a skillet or use a sandwich press.

5. Grill sandwiches 2–3 minutes on each side until cheese is melted and bread is golden. Griddle should not be too hot. Sandwiches should be cooked to about ⅓ of their original sizes. Slice sandwiches in half and serve.

Shredded Chicken

Cuban cooks often use pressure cookers to prepare food. A pressure cooker is a large cooking pot with a tightly-fitting lid that traps steam inside during the cooking process to enhance the food's flavors. Many American cooks prefer to use slightly smaller pots with high sides and lids called Dutch ovens. This Cuban dish, usually made with beef, earned the name Ropa Vieja (which means 'old clothes' in Spanish) because it resembles torn threads of worn fabric.

Ingredients for chicken

3   pounds boneless chicken breast
1   onion, cut in half
½   green pepper, cut into 2 parts

Ingredients for sauce

3   tablespoons cooking oil
1   medium onion, cut into thin slices
1   tablespoon minced garlic
½   green pepper, cut into thin slices
½   cup dry cooking wine
¼   teaspoon cumin
¼   teaspoon oregano
½   6-ounce can tomato paste
1   tablespoon chicken bouillon
10   pimento-stuffed olives

Directions

1. Have **an adult** boil meat with onion and green pepper in 8 cups water in Dutch oven. Cover and cook for 3 hours or until meat is tender. Cool and pull apart with a fork or with hands. (Make sure to wash them thoroughly first.) Keep broth and set aside.

2. Have an adult heat oil in a deep skillet. Add onions, garlic, and green peppers. Sauté until onions are transparent.
3. Add chicken and rest of ingredients. Stir constantly.
4. Add 1 cup broth. Lower heat, cover, and simmer for 15 minutes.
5. Serve with rice.

Chicken Spread

Cumin is a seasoning that comes from the seeds of an herb in the parsley family. It is used in cooking to give food a slightly peppery flavor. Cumin seeds can be used whole or ground. This simple, yet tasty dish is great to serve at parties or for a quick summer lunch.

Ingredients

2   cups chicken, cubed and cooked
⅓   cup mayonnaise
8   ounces cream cheese
½   teaspoon ground cumin
1   teaspoon minced garlic
½   cup sweet onion, minced
½   cup chopped black olives
½   cup chopped green olives

Directions

1. Place chicken, mayonnaise, cream cheese, and cumin in a food processor and process until coarsely chopped.
2. Place mixture in a large mixing bowl. Gently mix in garlic, onion, and all olives. Serve with crackers.

Cumin is a seasoning with a slight peppery flavor that is a popular addition to chicken recipes.

Imperial
Rice

This elegant dish is popular at parties because the shredded chicken serves more people than dishes with large pieces such as traditional arroz con pollo. Don't worry about the long list of ingredients! This recipe can be created in just an hour.

Ingredients

2   large cans cooked chicken or 1 whole chicken, cooked and deboned
2   cups cooked rice
2   tablespoons bacon bits
1½ cups white onion, finely chopped
2   cups green pepper, deseeded and chopped
3   green onions, trimmed and chopped
1   teaspoon oregano
3   teaspoons garlic granules
1   15-oz can tomato sauce
½   cup frozen green peas, cooked
⅓   cup mayonnaise
1   teaspoon lime juice
1   cup mild white cheese, grated
    Parmesan cheese to sprinkle
    red pepper slices
    green olives

Directions

1. Have **an adult** preheat oven to 325°F.
2. Have **an adult** heat a skillet over low heat. Drain chicken from cans, then cook chicken, bacon bits, onion, green pepper, green onion, and oregano for a few minutes in pan

until onion is clear. Add garlic and cook for an additional minute, stirring occasionally.

3. Add tomato sauce and chicken and bring to boil. Reduce heat to low and simmer, uncovered, for approximately 15 minutes to thicken sauce.

4. Add peas and lime juice during last 5 minutes of cooking. Set aside.

5. Add mayonnaise gradually to cooked rice, mixing thoroughly.

6. Take ⅓ of the rice and cover bottom of a 9 x 13-inch non-stick pan.

7. Layer chicken mixture on top of rice.

8. Add a layer of rice mixture.

9. Generously sprinkle Parmesan cheese on top of this layer.

10. Add remaining rice. Sprinkle Parmesan cheese on top layer, spreading cheese completely over top.

11. Bake 20 minutes or until cheese melts completely and bubbles, browning slightly.

12. Top with red pepper slices and green olives. Serve immediately.

Havana Punch

Parties are an important part of the Cuban culture. Cubans celebrate birthdays, anniversaries, holidays, and more—almost any event is deserving of a party! Families are included in the celebrations and children's tastes are accommodated with recipes they enjoy.

Ingredients

1 cup water
¼ cup honey
¼ cup sugar substitute
2 cinnamon sticks
4 whole cloves
1½ cups fresh pineapple juice
2 cups fresh orange juice
¼ cup lime juice
1 quart lemon sherbet
   (softened for 30 minutes at
   room temperature)
2 cups cold ginger ale

Lemon sherbet

Directions

1. Have **an adult** boil water in 1 quart saucepan.
2. Stir in honey and sugar substitute.
3. Add cinnamon sticks and cloves, stirring thoroughly.
4. Reduce heat to medium low and cook for 25 minutes uncovered until slightly thickened. Remove syrup from heat and let cool to room temperature.
5. Remove cinnamon sticks and whole cloves and place in refrigerator to chill.
6. Put juices and softened sherbet in large punch bowl and stir together. Add spiced syrup and ginger ale. Serve immediately over ice.

Havana Punch uses ingredients common to
Cuba like pineapple and orange juices.

Piña Colada

Pineapples are great in many recipes, including fruit salads and drinks. The interior of this oddly constructed fruit is chewy but tender, juicy, and fragrant. The coconut is the fruit of the coconut palm, a plant that is a primary food source throughout the tropics. Cuban cooking uses coconut milk often in puddings and desserts. Using fresh ingredients in recipes is preferred, but if you don't have time to extract the juices from the fruits, you can buy frozen or canned juices for quick, tasty results.

Ingredients

4   ounces fresh pineapple juice
4   ounces coconut cream, sweetened
    crushed ice
½   cup milk

Directions

1. Have **an adult** place all ingredients in blender and blend on high until thick and frozen. Serve immediately.

Mango and Papaya Milkshake

A mango is a tropical fruit with sweet, juicy, yellow flesh. If using fresh fruit, prepare the mango by having an adult carefully cut lengthwise slits through its skin. Tear skin away from the fruit in strips until all the peel is removed. Cut the flesh, removing the large flat seed in the center of the fruit. To prepare papaya, have an adult use a vegetable peeler to remove the skin. Cut fruit in half lengthwise, and use a spoon to scoop out small black seeds and stringy fruit. Dice the flesh. If fresh fruit is not available for this drink, you can purchase canned varieties. This refreshing tropical fruit drink can be a healthy and satisfying end to a meal.

Ingredients

1 cup diced mango, fresh or canned
1 cup diced papaya, fresh or canned
1–2 tablespoons sugar substitute
1 cup cold milk
⅔ cup crushed ice

Directions

1. Have **an adult** place all ingredients in a blender. Purée until smooth and frosty.
2. Pour into tall glasses and serve immediately.

Praline Coffee Soufflé

Sugar cane has been a staple crop in Cuba for generations. Desserts like Praline Coffee Soufflé utilize it and coffee—another Cuban crop.

Ingredients

3   eggs, yolks and whites separated
2½ tablespoons sugar substitute
2   packages unflavored gelatin
1   tablespoon instant coffee
     whipped cream
3   tablespoons Nutella®

Directions

1. Wrap wax paper around the outside of two small bowls with high sides and secure with tape. The paper should stand at least 1 inch above the tops of the bowls.
2. Beat egg yolks with sugar substitute until pale yellow.
3. Melt gelatin in 4 tablespoons of hot water in a mixing bowl. Stir in coffee.
4. Add egg and sugar substitute mixture, then gently fold in whipped cream and Nutella®.
5. In a separate bowl, whisk egg whites until they form stiff peaks. Fold into soufflé mixture. Carefully pour into prepared bowls.
6. Chill in refrigerator for 1 hour.
7. When ready to serve, remove paper, place spoonful of whipped cream on top of each soufflé and serve.

Praline coffee soufflé is an eye-catching and economical dessert.

Arroz con Leche
(Rice Pudding)

It is worth the time to prepare this recipe. It can be served warm or chilled. Have an adult use a potato peeler to gently remove the peel in small strips from the lemon. Try to avoid the white pith (inside of the rind) which has a bitter taste. This is the perfect ending to any Cuban meal!

Ingredients

½   cup uncooked white
        or brown rice
1½ cups water
1   lemon rind
1   cinnamon stick
5   cups whole milk
1   teaspoon vanilla extract
1¼ cups sugar substitute
        ground cinnamon
        raisins (optional)

Directions

1. Cook rice according to package directions with water, lemon rind, and cinnamon stick until soft.
2. Remove lemon rind and cinnamon stick and drain off excess water from rice (most of it will already have absorbed into rice).
3. Add milk, vanilla extract, and sugar substitute to rice. Cook over low heat, uncovered, stirring occasionally until thick for about 45 minutes. As the mixture thickens, stir more frequently to prevent burning and sticking.
4. Sprinkle with cinnamon and serve.

Flan
(Cuban Custard)

Flan is a rich egg custard with a Spanish origin. The flan is baked in custard cups or a shallow baking dish. This dish is then placed on a rack in a metal cake or jelly-roll pan filled with an inch or two of water. The water bath is called a *Bano de Maria*. The water bath prevents the bottom of the flan from burning. What makes flan special is not only the taste but its magic—the custard filling is poured into a pan that has been coated with dark caramelized sugar substitute. Once baked in the oven the caramel liquefies to create a delicious thin syrup.

Ingredients
4   cups milk
1   cinnamon stick
¼   cup sugar substitute
⅓   cup sugar substitute
3   eggs
4   egg whites (or ½ cup no cholesterol real egg product)
2   teaspoons vanilla extract

Directions
1. Have **an adult** preheat oven to 350°F.
2. Have **an adult** heat milk over low heat in saucepan and bring to boil, stirring constantly with cinnamon stick.
3. Remove milk from heat and let stand for 15 minutes. Remove cinnamon stick after milk cools.
4. To make caramel: Heat ¼ cup sugar substitute in bottom of skillet at medium-high heat until it begins to melt. Stir constantly to prevent burning. The sugar substitute will turn to thick syrup with a light brown color.
5. Quickly remove sugar substitute from heat and pour into flat dish or small cups. The syrup will harden quickly as it cools to form a shell.

Although it requires patience to make a delicious flan, the results are worth it!

6. Beat all eggs with ⅓ cup sugar substitute until thoroughly mixed and slightly frothy. Stir in warm milk mixture. Strain mixture through sieve (strainer). (Straining will result in smoother flan.)
7. Pour into caramel-lined dishes and set in large ovenproof baking dish with 1 inch of water in bottom. Take care that none of the boiling water in the bath gets into the dish or the custard will be spoiled.
8. Carefully place both pans into oven and bake for 50 minutes (reduce time by 5–10 minutes if you use small dishes). A knife inserted into each center should come out clean. Remove dishes from oven and allow flan to cool.
9. Before serving, have an adult loosen sides of flan dish with a knife. Have **the adult** flip the flan onto a rimmed platter. Spoon caramel syrup over each serving. If serving in individual custard cups, let flan cool and sprinkle with cinnamon for color.

Books

Behnke, Alison and Victor Manuel Valens. *Cooking the Cuban Way.* Lerner Publications Company: Minneapolis, MN, 2004.

Julien, Ronni. *The Everything Cooking for Kids Cookbook.* Adams Media: Avon, MA, 2010.

Legge, Anne. *Veggie Friends and Fruits Too! A Children's Cookbook on Creating Healthy Snacks.* BookSurge Publishing: Prescott, AZ, 2008.

Pavina, Erin. *Vegan Family Favorites: Tasty and Satisfying Recipes Even Your Kids Will Love.* VegFamily: Las Vegas, NV, 2005.

Stern, Michelle. *The Whole Family Cookbook.* Adams Media: Avon, MA, 2011.

Warner, Penny. *Healthy Snacks for Kids.* Bristol Publishing Enterprises: Hayward, Canada, 2007.

Zinczenko, David. *Eat This, Not That! for Kids! Thousands of Simple Food Swaps That Can Save Your Child from Obesity!* Rodale Publishing: Emmaus, PA, 2008.

Works Consulted:

Estefan, Emilio, and Gloria Estefan. *Estefan Kitchen.* New York: Celebra, 2008.

Lindgren, Glenn, Raul Musibay, and Jorge Castillo. *Three Guys from Miami Cook Cuban.* Salt Lake City, UT: Gibbs Smith, 2004.

Llamas, Beatriz. *A Taste of Cuba.* New York: Interlink Books, 2005.

Machado, Eduardo, and Michael Domitrovich. *Tastes like Cuba: An Exile's Hunger for Home.* New York: Gotham Books, 2007.

Roque, Raquel Rábade. *The Cuban Kitchen.* New York: Alfred A. Knopf, 2011.

Rose, Andy, and Judy Bastyra. *Eat Cuban.* London: Simon & Schuster, 2008.

On the Internet

Cuban Recipes
    http://www.food.com/recipes/cuban/popular
Introducing Cuba
    http://www.lonelyplanet.com/cuba,
Taste of Cuba, Cuban Restaurant Guide
    http://www.tasteofcuba.com/classic-cuban-cookbook.html,
Three Guys from Miami, Everything You Always Wanted to Know
    About Cuban and Spanish Food (But were afraid to ask!)
    http://3guysfrommiami.com/food.html

An orange seller

cilantro (sih-LAHN-troh)—Spice used to season many Latin American dishes.

clove (KLOHV)—Dried flower bud of a tropical tree, used whole or ground as a spice.

Communism (KOM-yoo-niz-uhm)—Method of holding all property in common.

cumin (KYOO-min)—Seed of a plant of the parsley family sold whole or ground and used in many Cuban dishes and sauces.

flan (FLAHN)—Rich egg custard baked in shallow baking dish coated with dark caramel; placed on a rack in a metal cake or jelly-roll pan filled with an inch of water to avoid burning.

mango—Oblong, sweet tropical fruit with yellow flesh eaten raw or canned.

medianoche (meh-dee-uh-NOH-chay)—Spanish word for "midnight;" A sandwich with this nickname contains the same ingredients as a Cuban sandwich but is made on a sweet bread called challah.

mince (MINTZ)—To cut or chop into small pieces.

oregano (uh-REG-uh-noh)—An herb of the mint family with leaves used as seasoning in cooking.

Organoponicos (or-gan-uh-PON-ih-kohs)—Garden located inside of a city; this type of agriculture was developed in Cuba in the 1950s during food shortages.

papaya (puh-PAH-yuh)—Large, yellow melon-like fruit of a tropical shrub or small tree.

ration (RAH-shun)—Fixed allowance of food during a shortage.

sugar cane—Tall tropical grass with a stout stalk. It changed the course of Cuban history when it was brought to the country to be harvested centuries ago. Its sugar and juice are extracted by crushing the stems.

yuca (YUHK-uh)—A root vegetable, also called cassava, used to thicken dishes.

About the AUTHOR

Kayleen Reusser is author of nine books for young readers. She works in a middle school library and enjoys speaking to children and adults about being an author. This is Reusser's second cookbook for children. She loves working with children and asked her young friends for advice when testing every recipe in this book. They all declared the dishes to be tasty! You can check out Reusser's web site at www.KayleenR.com.